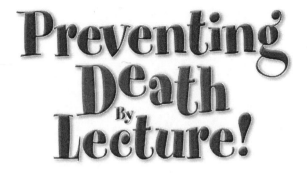

Preventing Death By Lecture!

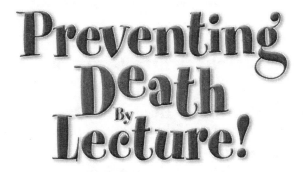

Preventing Death By Lecture!

Terrific Tips For Turning Listeners Into Learners

SHARON BOWMAN

Bowperson Publishing Company
Glenbrook, Nevada

Preventing Death By Lecture!

Terrific Tips For Turning Listeners Into Learners

Sharon L. Bowman, M.A.

Published by: **Bowperson Publishing Co.**
P.O. Box 564, Glenbrook, NV 89413
775-749-5247

Artwork by: Peter Janzen
Peter S. Janzen Art & Design
Fontana, Wisconsin 262-275-2910

Cover and text layout by: **Ad Graphics, Inc.**
Tulsa, Oklahoma 800-368-6196

Printed in the United States of America.

ISBN: 0-9656851-5-2

For Ross,
who thinks up
fabulous book titles,
And Mom,
who makes me
feel so good
about what I do.

DEDICATION AND PRAYER OF A LECTURE VICTIM:

This book is dedicated to
all of us who have experienced
the following excruciating demises:

**_Death by slide presentations,
death by speeches with overheads,
and death by lecture._**

May our executioners
read this book, see the light,
and resurrect their lectures and presentations.

May they keep their audiences alive and awake
with learner-centered activities
that infuse energy and interest.

**_And then may we all liven up our lectures
with terrific teaching tips
that celebrate learning – and life!_**

Contents

*Asked by his teacher
to summarize the life of
Socrates in four sentences,
the student said:
Socrates lived a long time ago.
He was very intelligent.
Socrates gave long speeches.
His listeners poisoned him.*

Anonymous

What's in It for YOU?

You KNOW there's a better way
to present information to your listeners
than straight lecture.

So you've spruced up your talk
with beautiful, high-tech computer slides
complete with all the bells and whistles.

But when all is said and done,
you realize that,
even with the cool-looking, multi-media fun,
your delivery is STILL lecture.

So WHAT do you do to involve your listeners?

HOW do you encourage them to learn
without wasting time?

What kinds of strategies do you use
to make sure your listeners
not only HEAR what you have to say,
but LEARN, REMEMBER, and USE it?

**If you want to make your lectures
learner-centered, interactive, and unforgettable,
this book is for YOU!**

WHY LECTURE?

But still his tongue ran on,
the less of weight it bore
with greater ease.

Samuel Butler

Are you ready for the million-dollar question?

Why is lecture STILL the most frequently
used method of delivering information?

How many reasons can you think of? List them in
your head and then check them against the list below.

Lecture is STILL the most frequently used method of
delivering information because:

➤ It's easier and more efficient for the lecturer;

➤ It has been modeled for us over and over again
by our families, schools, churches, and culture;

➤ It works for the strong auditory learners (those
who always remember what they hear the first
time they hear it);

➤ It's more organized – from the talker's point of
view;

➤ It means less preparation time for the speaker;

➤ It allows the one talking to be in control of the teaching;

➤ It's an old tradition – it has always been done that way;

➤ It's what's expected by the learners;

➤ It saves time when covering a large amount of information;

➤ Sometimes it's the only way to get the information across;

➤ It's an ego-boost for the lecturer.

And here's one more reason contributed by corporate trainer and president of Workshops by Thiagi, Sivasailam "Thiagi" Thiagarajan: *"On Abraham Maslow's hierarchy of human needs, right there above the needs for food, shelter, and sex, is the need to lecture!"* If you are a parent, you know what Thiagi means!

I'm not suggesting that you throw out all your lecture material. It's not an either/or proposition. Sometimes lecture is truly the best teaching strategy to use, given the time constraints, material, environment, and audience. However, most people only remember about 20% of what they hear. So if you want them to remember more than that, **you will involve them in the learning**. It's that simple.

FROM LISTENING TO LEARNING

A yawn is nature's way of giving
the person listening to a speaker
an opportunity to open his mouth.

Gian Vincenzo Gravina

A corporate trainer once told me that her courses were "highly interactive." She invited me to sit in on one of her classes. She had a whiz-bang PowerPoint presentation that certainly was entertaining. Through it all, her listeners sat passively watching the screen – no talking, no activity, no movement, no interaction.

Now I know she meant well, but her definition of "interactive" was certainly not MY definition of "interactive." I realized that, until we both understood what the other meant, we couldn't talk about learner-centered training strategies at all.

For the purposes of this book, "interactive" does NOT mean multi-media animation and sounds. "Learner-centered" does NOT mean that learners stare at interesting things on a screen. Here are the "Bowmanized" definitions you'll need to know in order to get the most out of this book:

"Hands-on" means that listeners are DOING something, as opposed to just sitting and listening.

"Interactive" means that listeners are talking to each other, participating in activities with each other, and learning FROM each other.

"Learner-centered" means that the focus is off you and is on your listeners. It means that your lecture includes time for your listeners to SAY and DO something with the information – which will help them REMEMBER and USE what they've just heard.

In other words,
your listeners become learners.

They become actively involved in their own learning – by talking about it, doing something with it, teaching it to others.

I'm not saying that you're doing it wrong. In fact, you're probably quite good at teaching others – you wouldn't be doing it if you weren't. All I'm saying is that you can make it work even better for your listeners if you add learner-involvement to your lecture.

Preventing Death by Lecture helps you make ANY lecture or presentation interactive and learner-centered. How? By using short, one-minute activities that get your listeners involved in their own learning in fun and memorable ways.

You don't have to change
your computer slides, your presentation script,
or your lecture information.

All you have to do
is add one or two ideas
from this book
to what you already do well.

This book gives you a collection of terrific tips to choose from that will make YOUR listeners become learners. The tips are loosely organized into three parts: the beginning (opening) of your lecture, the middle, and the end (closing). Each terrific tip has from one to four bonus tips to try.

Furthermore, this book is meant to be a resource – one that you might quickly flip through to find a teaching idea here, a presentation strategy there – all in the space of a few minutes. You don't need to read it cover-to-cover. You can skip around, flagging or highlighting the activities that appeal to you or your listeners the most.

If making your lecture more learner-centered is a new concept to you, never fear! Just choose one simple tip from this book that you feel you would be comfortable trying. Familiarize yourself with the instructions – maybe even practice saying them a few times. Then use the activity in your next talk.

After you and your listeners get used to one activity, vary it with another tip from this book. Or use these ideas to jump-start some of your own.

Use this book to help your listeners
not only HEAR your lecture,
but REMEMBER and USE it in their own lives.

THE TEN MINUTE RULE

*It's all right to hold a conversation,
but you should let go of it now and then.*

Richard Armour

Did you know that you're used to having information spoon-fed to you in eight-minute chunks? Do you know why? Of course you do – television!

If you're a normal TV watcher – and most of us are – you spend about two hours of your day in front of the television set. During that two hours, you watch at least 15 eight-minute chunks of information: eight minutes of sit-com, news, or a movie, followed by eight minutes (maybe more!) of commercials.

Now I'm not suggesting that you dummy-down your lesson or presentation material to accommodate our television culture. Nor am I suggesting that you limit the entire time you speak to just eight minutes.

Instead, you simply need to be aware of the shortened attention span of your learners and plan accordingly. That means that every eight – ten minutes (I round off to ten because it's easier for me to remember and to keep track of my time) you stop for a minute or two, **and involve your learners in a quick review of the information you just presented.**

Each time you stop, you review the information in a different way to keep your learners alert and interested. The pause can be as short as thirty seconds or as long as four minutes. **During the pause, your learners are involved in a quick, fun review of the material you've presented.** After the pause, you continue with your lecture – until another ten minutes has passed.

* * * * * * * * * * * * * * * * * * *

Bonus Idea: The Twenty Minute Rule

Can't seem to stop after ten minutes? Then aim for twenty or thirty minutes at first – until you're comfortable building short, learner-centered activities into your lecture or presentation. Remember though, *the longer you talk, the easier it is for them to forget what you've said!*

Bonus Idea: Time It

Don't know when ten or twenty minutes have elapsed? Think you've only been talking for ten minutes when in fact it's been about forty-five? Set a quiet timer or assign someone to signal you with a time sign (a handwritten sign, a capital "T" made with his/her hands, etc.) so that you can learn to gauge the time you've been speaking. After awhile, you won't need the timer or time signal.

BEGINNING WITH CONNECTIONS

BEGINNING WITH CONNECTIONS

Education is not the filling of a pail,
But the lighting of a fire.

William Butler Yeats

What are the two most powerful teaching moments in your lecture? If you said the beginning and the end, you're absolutely correct!

As a learner, you usually remember the beginning and end of events, stories, and a learning experience. While you may often forget the middle of something, the beginning and end most often stick out in your mind.

For you as a giver of information, then, it becomes important to create a memorable beginning (opening) and end (closing) to your presentation.

Many folks start with a story (topic-related, of course). A story is a great teaching tool: it creates a mental picture that listeners remember – especially if you liven up the story with props, dialogue, movement, visuals, etc. The only downside to a story is this: *YOU are still doing all the talking; your listeners are still doing just that – listening.*

Now don't leave your stories out – use them. AND, in addition to a story, include something that will be even more memorable to your listeners: ***involve them in the opening.***

The first six terrific tips in this book are opening ideas to play with. Choose one and use it in your next talk. If you're not used to involving your listeners in an activity at the beginning, choose the idea that is the easiest and most comfortable for you to include.

All these tips have the following in common:

➤ They are fun, memorable ways of opening your lecture;

➤ They connect your listeners to each other, thus creating a feeling of psychological safety and trust among the group (safety is a crucial part of successful learning);

➤ They connect your listeners to the topic – and to what they already know about the topic (this "linking" of old information to the new is also crucial to learning);

➤ They keep listeners interested, involved, and more energized.

The bottom line?
Don't change a word of your opening –
just add a short learner-centered piece to it.
This is the first step for turning
listeners into learners.

EXPERTS UNITE!

(Activity time: 2 minutes)

This is my standard opening activity, no matter what the topic and what the teaching format: class lecture, keynote address, speech, presentation, or training.

I begin by saying:

"There are some folks in this room who are crucial to your learning. They already know a lot about the topic – in fact, a few of them are experts and could be up here talking to you instead of me. Look to your left, to your right, and in front and behind you. You'll find the experts sitting there. Take ninety seconds right now to introduce yourself to them and to find out one fact about the topic that they already know. This is your 'Expert Group.'"

After the ninety seconds are up, and if you can spare another minute or two, you might ask for a few volunteers to share one fact they heard someone in their expert groups say. Or you can just summarize

23

the activity by reminding your learners that, during your presentation, they will simply add to what they already know about the topic.

Here is a reminder of what you just did and why you did it:

➤ You quickly connected your learners to each other and to the topic you're presenting;

➤ You created a bridge or link from what they know to what you'll be teaching them;

➤ You provided a psychologically safe learning environment for the folks who are present. They will be more open to the learning and more willing to take risks (like asking questions!);

➤ You honored them by showing them that you value what they already know about the topic.

* * * * * * * * * * * * * * * * * * *

Bonus Tip: Learning Buddies

Another way to begin is to say: *"Learning is not a spectator sport. There are four people crucial to your successful learning during this presentation. They are your learning buddies and they are sitting to your left, right, in front, and behind you. Take a few seconds to introduce yourself to your learning buddies and find out one thing they want to learn from today's presentation."*

Bonus Tip: Shout Out

After the expert group members or learning buddies have finished their introductions and discussion, do a quick "Shout Out" (see Tip # 10) with the whole group.

TAKE A GUESS

(Activity time: 3 minutes)

At the beginning of your lecture, tell your learners to pair up (triads are okay too, so that no one is left out) and, with their partners, create a list of 3-6 important facts about the topic that they think you will cover in your presentation. While you talk, they circle any items on their lists that you mention. They can also add facts to their lists as directed by you.

When you finish your presentation, and if you have the time, you can ask for a few volunteers to tell the whole group what they feel is the most important fact on their lists.

Again, you're keeping your learners alert, interested, and motivated to listen.

You've focused their minds on what they know and on what you want them to know.

* * * * * * * * * * * * * * * * * * *

Bonus Tip: Guess Again

After you finish speaking, instruct your learners to refer to their lists once again to see if there are any facts they wrote down that you didn't talk about. They can take a guess as to why you didn't include this information. They can ask you about these items.

Or you can tell them that this information will be covered in part two of your talk!

Bonus Tip: Cartoon Caper

David Meier, director of The Center for Accelerated Learning, did the following brilliant variation of this activity:

Before he began his one-hour presentation on accelerated learning, Dave passed out note-taking sheets to the participants. On each paper was a series of three-four cartoons down the left side of the page, a blank space down the middle, and another series of cartoons down the right side of the paper.

Dave explained that the left-side cartoons illustrated points about old ways of teaching and the right-side cartoons illustrated the new teaching models he was going to talk about.

Dave asked the participants to stand, pair up, and take about three minutes to guess the points he was going to make based on the old/new teaching methods as illustrated by the cartoons.

After three minutes, Dave directed his audience to sit down and take notes in the middle blank portion of the paper. He paused during his presentation and asked for a show of hands as to which people guessed his cartoons correctly.

The cartoons provided visual cues for the presentation points. The participants all wanted to check their own accuracy in guessing, so they listened intently through the entire lecture. The note-taking page became a review and "souvenir" to take with them when Dave finished his talk.

CHEATING ALLOWED

(Activity time: 3 – 4 minutes)

Want to challenge your learners before you begin your talk? Give each person a worksheet you've created beforehand – one that lists about a dozen questions pertaining to your presentation. Make the questions difficult enough so that your learners won't know some/all the answers (after all, that's why they are there – to LEARN the answers from YOU!).

Direct them to stand, walk around the room, ask other people what they think the answers are, and then write the answers on the paper.

At the end of the time allotted, call for their attention, thank them, and have them sit down. Then tell them to listen for the answers as you talk. They can circle the right answers and cross out or change the wrong ones on their papers.

Again, you've focused their attention on what you want them to know, and they'll listen with that purpose in mind.

* * * * * * * * * * * * * * * * * * * *

Bonus Tip: Pre and Post

Use the worksheet as a pre- and post-assessment tool. After your presentation, have the learners do the worksheet again and see how much they improved and how much they now know the second time around.

Bonus Tip: Fill-in-the-Blanks

Instead of listing questions, list facts pertaining to your lecture but leave out important key words in each fact/sentence. Learners try to fill in the missing words before your lecture. Then, during your presentation, they listen for the missing words and change the ones they filled in incorrectly, or fill in the ones they didn't know.

Bonus Tip: Look It Up

If you use handout materials, learners can search for answers or fill-ins by using the written materials in addition to or instead of asking others.

Bonus Tip: Fill-in-the-Squares

Instead of a list of questions, post a list (where everyone can see it) of important facts related to the topic. Direct the learners to fold a blank paper into 6 squares (8, 10 – the number is determined by you). Learners write one fact in each square (tell them they can choose the facts they want to write – they don't need to go in order from the list). During your presentation, they circle or cross off the facts you cover. At the end of the talk, they check to see if they have all their facts circled. If not, they can ask you or another person about the missing items.

NIFTY NOTES

(Activity time: 30 seconds to 1 minute)

Here is a great way to keep your learners focused while you speak – and to give them an opportunity to create a different kind of "souvenir" to take with them to review later.

Before beginning your lecture, tell your learners to take out a blank piece of paper and divide it into four columns. At the top of each column they draw the following pictures:

➤ A book (for important facts)

➤ A light bulb (for the "ahas" or "new ideas")

➤ A question mark (for any questions they have)

➤ A running stick figure (for their "action plans")

While delivering your talk, stop at different times and tell them to write one word or phrase in one column. The first time you might say:

"In the book column, write one important fact you just learned ...

The next time you pause, you might say:

In the light bulb column write an idea that is brand new to you ...

Later say:

In the question mark column write a question you have ...

At the end of your presentation, say:

In the stick figure column write what you plan to do with this information."

If time allows, they can tell the person sitting next to them what they've written. Or a few people can tell the whole group what they wrote. Or you can simply continue with your message and answer a few of the questions at the end.

This kind of note-taking is called an "advanced organizer." Its benefits are many:

➤ It focuses the learners on what to pay attention to;

➤ It helps them organize and remember the information;

➤ It keeps them involved while listening;

➤ It allows for questions without interrupting the flow of the presentation;

➤ It becomes a review "souvenir" to read again after the lecture is over.

Contributor: Diane Cheatwood
Educational Consultant, CO

* *

Bonus Tip: Mind-Mapping

Instead of columns, learners write the topic in the middle of the paper and put facts, questions, comments, etc. in bubbles or geometric shapes around the topic. They connect the shapes to the topic with lines.

Mind-mapping is the creation of a spatial or visual "map" of information that helps learners remember more because they can visualize the placement of the words.

Bonus Tip: Flash Cards

Each learner receives a stack of index cards. During your lecture or presentation, learners write important facts, words, points, or questions on each card – one written item per card. After the presentation, they review their cards, compare cards with a neighbor, exchange cards, or ask their questions of each other or you. They take their cards with them when they leave.

TIE A YELLOW RIBBON

(Activity time: 30 seconds to 1 minute)

This is an unusual and delightful way to spark interest in your lecture or presentation.

Before you begin, give each learner a piece of colorful ribbon (about 6 inches in length).

As you cover an important point, tell learners to tie a knot in the ribbon and repeat the important point out loud with you. Or they can turn to the person sitting next to them and repeat the information.

Do this for the four – six most important points in your lecture.

At the end of your presentation, have learners pair up, touch each knot, and repeat each point out loud to their partners.

Like the Nifty Notes, these ribbons become review "souvenirs" of the points the learners need to remember.

Contributor: Kim Gordey, Canada

* * * * * * * * * * * * * * * * * * * *

Bonus Tip: Knotty Stuff

Instead of ribbon, use pieces of soft rope, colorful yarn, or other materials that feel and look interesting.

Your tactile learners (those who learn through the sense of touch) will love you for it!

Bonus Tip: Sticky Stuff

Learners write the important points on small post-it notes and then stick them to handout materials, to their clothes, or to a piece of colorful cardboard, construction paper, or poster-board.

Bonus Tip: Thematic Stuff

If your lecture revolves around a particular theme, tie (excuse the pun!) the "knot-able" material to the theme in some way. For example, learners could have pieces of artificial vine for a jungle theme, pieces of bendable, plastic-covered, electrical wire for a technology theme, or pieces of leather strips for an ecology theme.

Bonus Tip: Edible Stuff

How about those long strings of licorice? Learners could tie them in knots then eat what they've learned! Ah well, it was food for thought!

RED LIGHT, GREEN LIGHT

(Activity time: 30 seconds to 1 minute)

Anytime you give your learners something out of the ordinary, you spark their curiosity and interest. What you hand out to them can be as simple as two colored index cards.

Before beginning your presentation, give each learner a red and a green index card (other colors are fine too). Or use white index cards and learners can color their own with felt pens.

During your talk, ask a question and have learners raise the green card in the air if the answer is "yes," and the red card for "no." Then answer the question and continue with the presentation.

The cards can also stand for: agree/disagree, okay/ no way, love it/hate it, or anything you wish that pertains to the information you're presenting.

* * * * * * * * * * * * * * * * * * * *

Bonus Tip: Stoplight

Instead of cards, use pictures of a traffic signal with the red and green lights colored in. Add a third card with a yellow light that stands for: "Not sure about it ... need more time or more information."

Bonus Tip: Talk or Walk

You can use the cards to find out if the participants need a break or not. Say:

"Hold up your green card if you want me to continue with the presentation for a bit longer. Hold up your red card if you need a break right now."

Bonus Tip: Card-on-a-Stick

Glue the two cards to a tongue depressor stick (found in local craft stores). Each learner has a card-on-a-stick that can be turned for yes or no answers, for agree or disagree, etc. Or have learners make their own cards-on-sticks before the presentation.

Marking the Middle

Marking
the Middle

The less you talk,
the more you're listened to.
Abigail Van Buren

If the opening and closing are the two parts of your talk that learners will remember the most, what do you do about all that information in the middle?

You already know that you're going to involve your learners every ten minutes or so by breaking up your lecture with activities from this book.

You can also "mark the middle"
with mini-openings and closings.

You decide where to include a break in your talk and if that break signals the beginning of new topic-related information or the end of the information you've just covered. In other words, you choose a learner-centered activity for the break that would be a memorable mini-opening or mini-closing.

The following ten terrific tips serve these purposes:

➤ They are great short, quick, review activities;

> Most of them connect the learners to both the topic and each other again;

> Most of them can be a mini-opening or mini-closing activity.

If all this learner-centered stuff is new to you, then just choose one activity to use in the middle of your next lecture.

If this is old hat to you – your learners are actively involved every step of the way – then take an idea and see how many variations you can create from it.

Of course, you can always use one of the opening or closing activities in this book in the middle of your talk – in fact, you can use any of these ideas any way you wish! Just make sure you know WHAT you're doing and WHY! Better yet, *tell your learners what they're going to do and why they're going to do it.* You'll get more buy-in and most will join in with gusto!

NUDGE YOUR NEIGHBOR

(Activity time: 1 minute)

You've made your opening remarks. You've done an opening activity. You've been talking now for about ten to twenty minutes. You don't want to interrupt the flow of your lecture, but you know you need to stop and involve your learners in some way. So you do the activity that is the shortest, quickest, and easiest – the Neighbor Nudge. You say:

"It's your turn. Look at your neighbor – the person sitting to the left or right of you. Make sure no one is left out. Nudge your neighbor and tell him/her the most important fact you've just heard in the last ten to twenty minutes. Find out what your neighbor thinks is the most important fact. You have sixty seconds to talk to each other."

When the minute is up, resume your lecture. It's that simple.

Contributor: Neal Tardiff, CA

* * * * * * * * * * * * * * * * * * * *

Bonus Tip: Pair-Share

In **Presenting with Pizzazz** I call the "Neighbor Nudge" a "Pair-Share," and it can be done a dozen different ways so that you don't have to repeat the same procedure each time. It's a no-fail teaching tool that can work with any size group – and that automatically gets everyone involved in the learning.

Here are few of the many variations to the Pair-Share:

➤ Share one thing you just learned;

➤ Share on question you still have;

➤ State three things you now know that you didn't know before;

➤ Ask your neighbor a question about the topic and see if he/she can answer it;

➤ Tell your neighbor how you can use the information you just learned.

Bonus Tip: Welcome to the Neighborhood!

Each time you ask learners to nudge a neighbor, direct them to different partners: a person in front or behind them, a person sitting two seats away, a person with longer/shorter hair, a person with the same/different colored clothing, etc. Always remind them to make sure that no one is left out – triads are okay.

Bonus Tip: Talking about Talking

If you have the time, take one more minute to process the pairs discussions by asking for a few volunteers to tell the entire group what their neighbor considered important from the lecture. Then thank them and continue with your presentation.

Bonus Tip: Group Management Tool

Use a noisemaker (whistle, chime, bell, etc.), a raised hand, or a verbal or written announcement to quiet the group. Quickly turn the room lights on or off. Or ask everyone to clap (stomp, sing, raise hands in the air, etc.) with you until the whole group is doing it.

ALL TOGETHER NOW!

(Activity time: a few seconds)

During your lecture, you may have a list of bulleted points written on charts, overhead transparencies or slides, that you want your learners to remember.

Instead of you reading your bulleted points aloud, you're going to involve your learners in the verbal reading. You say:

"We all know that the person doing the most talking is doing the most learning. So if I read these points aloud all by myself, I'm mastering this information – but you aren't. However, when you read this information aloud with me, you master it too. And you'll remember it longer and be able to explain it to others. So please read the information aloud with me."

If they are reluctant to do so, read the bulleted point once, and ask them to read it aloud a second time. Once they get the idea, they'll read aloud with you – especially if you make it lighthearted and fun (how about saying it in a low voice, high voice, squeaky voice, growly voice?)

By doing this "choral reading,"
your learners not only SEE the information,
they also SAY it and HEAR it –
which helps them remember it longer.

* * * * * * * * * * * * * * * * * * * *

Bonus Tip: Whose Turn Is It?

Instead of directing everyone to read each point aloud, direct only certain people to read aloud each time:

People with hair longer than their shoulders, read this aloud ...

Only the males read this aloud ...

Only those wearing red read this aloud ...

Use some of the following – or make up your own:

➤ People with long hair/short hair;

➤ People who are male/female;

➤ People who are younger than/older than (name an age);

➤ People who are wearing red/blue/yellow/etc.

➤ People who are wearing a watch, earrings, etc.

➤ People who are from other states;

➤ People who were born in the winter/summer;

➤ People who have old/new shoes;

➤ People who have a long first/last name.

Bonus Tip: Chorus Line

If there is a point that you want repeated – or a bottom line to your presentation that deserves repetition, have the learners verbally say it, shout it, or whisper it each time the point comes up – like the chorus of a well-known song which everyone sings even if they don't know the verses.

Bonus Tip: And Ain't It So!

If the point is important enough, your learners read it aloud, turn to their neighbors, and say, "And ain't it so!" or some other humorous sentence that you invent to fit the information and occasion.

Signals

(Activity time: 30 seconds)

Y ou continue your lecture for another ten to twenty minutes. Now you stop and ask your learners if they agree or disagree with the points you've just made by showing you a "thumbs up" signal if they agree or "thumbs down" signal if they don't. Thumbs sideways can stand for "undecided" or "need more information."

Signals do three things:

➤ They keep your learners awake and interested;

➤ They give your kinesthetic learners (the ones who learn through physical movement) something to do;

➤ They help you check for understanding. If many learners show you the wrong signal, or if they seem unsure about what signal to use, you know that they didn't "get it" and you need to review what you just presented.

* * * * * * * * * * * * * * * * * * * *

Bonus Tip: Clap and Stomp

Use a variety of signals so that they don't get boring. Direct your learners to:

➤ Clap for "yes" and stomp for "no;"

➤ Shout "Of course!" for "yes" and "No way!" for "no;"

➤ Nod and shake heads for agree and disagree;

➤ Show the "okay" sign (thumb and forefinger circled) to signal agreement;

➤ Use the American Sign Language signals for "yes" (make a fist, knuckles up, and shake fist up and down like a nod), and "no" (make a fist, knuckles up, and then extend thumb and first two fingers and pat fingers against thumb).

Bonus Tip: Show Me

Make up your own signals that relate to your topic or that take care of group management needs. Some examples are:

➤ Have learners make a fist and circle it over their heads like a lasso if they didn't understand the information or if they want you to repeat something;

➤ Tell learners to touch a part of their own body (elbow, forehead, shoulder, etc.) and repeat a certain important fact (a different fact for each body part) – after a few repetitions, they will associate the body part with the information.

➤ If they need a break before you call for one, or if you have been lecturing too long and they need to move, have learners signal you with a time sign or shout "Break!" Better yet, give them permission to move around even when you're talking (kinesthetic learners will love you for this!)

➤ Create a signal that relates to information in your presentation and teach it to your learners. Then use the signal at various times throughout your talk to help them remember the information.

SHOUT OUT!

(Activity time: 1 – 2 minutes)

After another ten minutes or so of talking, stop and ask someone to shout out a number between five and ten (between any two numbers will do).

Say someone shouts out the number "seven." Now tell the whole group that it's their job to come up with seven facts about the topic that they've just learned (or seven facts about a certain topic point, seven things they remember from your lecture, seven bulleted points from your written information or slides, etc.) They shout out the facts and you count them until the number has been reached. Then you add any important pieces of information they may have forgotten – or correct any erroneous information. Have them give themselves a round of applause and continue with your presentation.

Bob Pike, corporate trainer and president of The Bob Pike Group, reminds us that:

Adults don't argue with their own data.

By having your learners verbally repeat the information you've taught them, they now own it – it's their information and no longer yours. They'll not only remember it longer, but they'll talk about it, teach it to others, and defend it if need be.

* * * * * * * * * * * * * * * * * * *

Bonus Tip: Pep Rally Shout Out

Just as a pep rally gets folks ready for a big game, the Pep Rally Shout Out lets learners review what they already know about a topic BEFORE your lecture. Follow the procedure above before you begin talking, so that they can express what they already know. This shows them that you value their knowledge.

Bonus Tip: Altogether Shout Out

If a certain point is really important, have the group shout it out with you – and intersperse the Shout Out throughout your lecture, repeating the same point so that they all will remember it forever!

Bonus Tip: The Out-the-Door Shout

At the end of your talk, use the Shout Out to remind your learners of the most important point of your lecture.

PASS THAT QUESTION

(Activity time: 3 – 5 minutes)

D id you know that, when questioning techniques are included in a lecture, the retention of information skyrockets?

This doesn't mean that you ask: *"Are there any questions?"* and then, when no one says anything, you continue your presentation.

It means that you use a number of different ways to get ALL your learners involved in creating and answering questions.

One method is to stop talking and say:

"You are now going to test the person on your right to see how smart he or she is. On an index card or scratch paper, write down a question that pertains to the information you've just heard. You must know the answer to your own question. Pass the card to the person on your right (folks sitting at the end of a row can pass the card to someone in another row or all the way down to the other end of his/her own row). Take a minute to read the question you've been passed and to write your own answer to it. Then they pass the card back to its original owner. Check the answer and let your neighbor know if he or she got it right."

* * * * * * * * * * * * * * * * * * * *

Bonus Tip: Pass That Answer

Instead of writing a question, learners write an answer to a question and the person on the right guesses what the question is and writes it on the card. Or they write an answer to a question you give them and then they compare their answers. You ask a few volunteers to state their answers and then you tell them if they were correct.

Bonus Tip: Pass It Again

Thiagi uses another high-interest questioning technique after about ten minutes of lecture:

Each learner writes a question or a fact just learned on an index card. Each passes her card to another person who then passes it again to someone else. The passing continues a few times until the questions are sufficiently mixed up. Then Thiagi asks a few volunteers to read the questions they have aloud and either he or the learners answer the questions.

You have to allow about 5 minutes for verbal processing if you do this. You can take as many or as few questions as time allows.

Bonus Tip: Collect That Question

Instead of passing the questions, you collect the cards and, during a break, skim them for the most important questions, which you address after the break. Again allow about 5 minutes to answer the ones you've chosen and to take any comments from the group.

THINK AND WRITE

(Activity time: 1 minute)

Stop your lecture and ask the learners to take out a piece of scratch paper and jot down their own reactions, thoughts, ideas, or questions about your talk. After about one minute of writing, you resume your presentation – or you can take another minute to have a few volunteers share what they've written with the whole group.

By doing this, you're allowing your learners to mentally process the information a second time.

This deepens their understanding of the material you just presented.

* * * * * * * * * * * * * * * * * * *

Bonus Tip: Doodle It

Instead of writing a phrase or sentence, learners draw a quick doodle representing something about what they just learned. Also called an "analog drawing," the doodle is a visual representation of information because learners often remember pictures longer than words. Tell the group that this is not an art contest – their doodles can simply be lines, shapes, forms, whatever. If they wish, they can label their doodles afterwards.

Bonus Tip: The Sound of Music

During the writing or doodling, play quiet music (about 60-80 beats per minute, no vocals) in the background. This helps most learners enter into a relaxed, receptive state of concentration.

Bonus Tip: It's Marginal

If learners have a handout or workbook, they can jot down their responses to the information in the margins on the pages. They can also draw their doodles in the margins.

STAND UP, SIT DOWN

(Activity time: 2 – 4 minutes)

If your learners have been sitting for a long while, it's time to get them up and moving. Direct them to form standing cluster groups of 3-5 people (or they can stand with their expert groups).

Each person in the standing groups tells the others one thing they remember or have just learned from the presentation. That person then sits down. The activity continues until everyone in each group is seated. Call time after about four minutes, even if some groups haven't finished.

By balancing sitting with standing,
you are making sure that your learners
stay physically awake and alert.

This will also help them to remember your information longer.

* * * * * * * * * * * * * * * * * *

Bonus Tip: Questioning Bee

Have the entire group stand in place. Then ask them a question pertaining to the information you've just presented. Make the question difficult enough that many will not know the answer. Direct them to tell a neighbor what they think the answer is. Then tell them the right answer. All those who answered it correctly remain standing. Those who didn't have the correct answer sit down. Repeat the procedure one or two more times until only a few people remain standing. Have the seated people give the standing ones a round of applause – or hand out small, inexpensive prizes.

Bonus Tip: Hands Down

The whole group stands up. Direct them to raise their hands in the air with you. While their hands are raised, ask them a question. Tell them to drop their hands when you drop yours, and shout out their answers (they'll all shout at the same time). Then tell them the correct answer and direct those who got it to sit down. Do the activity one or two more times until everyone is seated. Then have them give themselves a round of applause and resume your lecture.

Bonus Tip: You Bet Your Life

Ask a question related to the information you just presented. If your question is moderately easy to answer, say:

"Please stand if you're absolutely sure you know the answer – and you would bet your life on it."

Then have the standing people explain to the sitting people around them their answers. After that, tell the whole group your answer.

If your question is a moderately difficult one, say:

"Please stand if you're pretty sure you know the answer – but you wouldn't bet your life on it."

"Stand if you not only know the answer but could come up here and teach it to the group."

"Stand if you not only don't know the answer, but you don't think that I know what I'm talking about either."

MICRO-MACRO STRETCHES

(Activity time: 1 – 3 minutes)

L et's really go for it now! Maybe your learners have just eaten a meal, or maybe it's early morning or evening – whatever! Your learners need a big dose of physical movement immediately, but you don't want to waste any of your lecture time on an activity that doesn't have anything to do with the topic. So you do the following:

Explain to the group that micro stretches mean moving a small part of the body (example: a finger, toe, mouth, eye, etc.) Macro stretches mean moving a large part of the body (leg, arm, torso, etc.).

Direct the group to stand. Tell them you will model a micro or macro stretch and they are to do it with you. While everyone stretches, you verbally state one fact you covered that's topic-related.

Then you call on another person in the group to model a micro or macro stretch. While the group repeats the stretch with that person, he/she states another fact learned about the topic.

That person then calls on someone else – or you can do the naming. After three or four micro/macro stretches, the group sits down and you continue the lecture.

*Again, when you include
physical movement in the review,
your learners stay
both physically and mentally alert.*

* * * * * * * * * * * * * * * * * *

Bonus Tip: Jumping Jacks

Direct everyone to stand and to do the first move of a jumping jack (legs apart, arms stretched overhead, palms of hands together – you model it). Then tell them they can't move until someone shouts out one important thing they just learned. When that happens, direct them to do the second move of a jumping jack (legs together, arms and hands by sides). Repeat the procedure three or four times while reviewing important facts from your talk.

Bonus Tip: Running in Place

Learners stand and run in place while telling their neighbors the most important things they just learned. When done, they can sit down.

Bonus Tip: Moving and Mirroring

Learners stand and pair up (triads are okay too – make sure no one is left out). One person is the "mover" and one person is the "mirror." The mover does a "slow-motion" move while the mirror follows the movement, doing it along with the mover. The mover states one fact or question pertaining to the topic. The mirror answers the question or states a fact relating to the first fact. Then the partners switch roles and do the moving/mirroring activity again.

<u>Go Fish</u>

(Activity time: 1 – 2 minutes)

This activity is a great review if you have learners seated in groups at tables.

Before your lecture, create and distribute small jars, boxes, or bags (one per table), filled with paper strips on which you've written important questions or facts about the topic.

Every ten minutes you stop talking and tell the table groups to choose one strip from their jar. The person who chooses the strip reads it to the table group and then the group must either answer the question or explain why the fact is important. If the question or fact is one you haven't covered yet, they put it back in the jar and choose another one.

If you have enough time, a few groups can report out to the entire group. Or simply call on one different group to report out each time they do the activity. The groups won't know which one you'll call on so all will make sure they have the answers.

Contributor: Tilloretta Pope
Community College of Aurora, CO

* * * * * * * * * * * * * * * * * * * *

Bonus Tip: Pick That Person

Instead of the table groups answering the question or explaining the fact, one person from each group chooses the paper slip, reads, and answers it. The table group then lets the person know if he/she was correct, or if they agree/disagree with the answer.

You can also pick the person at each table group by saying:

The person with the most pets chooses the next paper slip.

The person wearing the most jewelry chooses the next paper slip.

The person with the longest hair/shortest hair ...

The oldest/youngest person ...

The person wearing the brightest colors ...

The person with the longest middle name ...

Bonus Tip: Backyard Fishing

Each table group collectively and quickly writes two or three questions about the information just presented – one question per slip of paper or index card. Then each table group chooses one person to go to another table (their "backyard") and "fish for a question," i.e. choose a question slip from that table to bring back to the home table. Table groups collectively answer the question. If time allows, have some of the groups report out their questions and answers.

PASSING THE BUCK

(Activity time: 30 seconds to 1 minute)

After ten minutes of lecture, stop and ask for one question from a volunteer. Answer the question, thank the volunteer, and hand the person a dollar bill. Then continue with your talk.

The next time a question is asked, tell the first person to pass the dollar bill to the person asking the second question.

The dollar bill makes its way around the room as learners ask questions at specific times, as directed by you. The person who asks the last question gets to keep the dollar bill.

Contributor: Larry Forman
City College, CA

* * * * * * * * * * * * * * * * * * *

Bonus Tip: Pass the Potato

Instead of a dollar bill, use a vegetable, candy bar, or small toy or stuffed animal. If your presentation has a theme to it, make the object theme-related.

Bonus Tip: Money Madness

While you talk, learners continue to pass the dollar bill or object around the room. Remind them that they cannot hold onto it – they must pass it as soon as they get it. When you stop the lecture, you also tell them to stop passing the dollar or object. The person with it in his/her hand stands up. If he/she can answer your question, that person keeps the dollar bill or object. Then begin the activity again with a new dollar or object. Or just give the person a round of applause and use the same bill or object again.

CLOSING WITH CELEBRATION

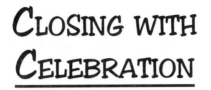

CLOSING WITH CELEBRATION

What we learn with pleasure we never forget.

Lewis Mercier

Your presentation is almost over. Your learners have listened to you and have talked with each other. They've written some notes and reviewed the material. You're wrapping up now. What's left?

An action plan –
connections again –
and celebration!

Before you make your closing remarks, invite your learners to think about what they plan to do with what they've learned. Also direct them to think about what they enjoyed most about the learning experience. Then have them connect with each other and your message one more time so that they leave feeling good about themselves and what they've learned from you.

The following four tips are great closing activities. Of course, you can also use them at other times during your lecture. As closing activities, these tips do the following:

➤ They reconnect learners to each other and to the topic;

➤ They help learners focus on an "action plan," i.e. what they plan to do with what they've learned;

➤ They create a moment of celebration – when learners applaud themselves and their learning;

➤ They provide a memorable end to your talk – and learners WILL remember your information because of the fun they had at the closing.

TOSS IT AROUND

(Activity time: 1 –3 minutes)

This is my all-time favorite closing activity. And it ALWAYS provides a high-energy note at the end of the presentation.

Announce that you have in your hand a "random response device" (Thiagi's label for something soft and throwable). The best object is a koosh ball, but you can also use a nerf ball, a bath net, a sponge, or a stuffed animal.

Let your learners know that, when they catch the ball, they need to tell the group two things:

➤ What they appreciated about the group or the learning experience;

➤ What they plan to do with what they learned.

Then they toss it to someone else. Remind them that it isn't a throwing/catching contest. It's a celebration activity. And tell them they can repeat what someone else has said (so that they aren't put on the spot if they can't think quickly on their feet).

The random response device is a group management tool that does the following:

➤ It gives more people an opportunity to talk;

➤ It keeps those who always talk from monopolizing the discussion;

➤ It gives a structure to the activity that keeps the answers short and fast-paced;

➤ It holds everyone's interest;

➤ It adds fun and humor to the activity.

If your group is large, limit the number of tosses to a half-dozen or so. Or invite those who wish to talk to raise their hands and toss the ball to them.

By using a ball toss at the end of your talk, you've helped your learners focus on what they enjoyed and their commitment to use what they learned.

You've also ended on a high note that will be remembered long after the learning is over.

* *

Bonus Tip: A Little or a Lot

Depending upon the time you have available, you can use the random response device to take as few as one or two comments or as many as ten or twelve. You control the duration of the activity and ask your learners to toss the ball to you when the time is up.

Bonus Tip: The Mouth

Give each "expert group" a small toy that represents "the mouth." Only the person with "the mouth" can speak. "The mouth" is then passed around the expert group to give everyone a chance to share their action plans and compliments.

Bonus Tip: Four or More

If you really want to keep things hopping, toss out four or more random response devices. The learners take turns shouting out their answers and tossing the objects to others.

ONE-LEGGED INTERVIEW

(Activity time: 1 minute)

This is a kinesthetic variation of the Neighbor Nudge – and a fun way to end a presentation.

Learners stand and pair up (triads are okay too so that no one is left out). One person is the interviewer and the other is the talker. The interviewer asks the talker what he/she plans to do with what was learned. The talker must stand on one leg while answering the question (this keeps the answer short and makes the interview fun). After about 30 seconds, they reverse roles and do the one-legged interview again. Then they give each other a high-five.

Pairs can also discuss what they enjoyed the most about the learning, who they plan to share it with, and a kudo for the group.

Humor is a wonderful learning aid. The One-Legged Interview, and all its variations, adds the ingredient of humor to your message. ***An extra value to humor is that folks generally want more of whatever it is that creates the smiles and laughter.*** So learning becomes a desirable thing to do.

* * * * * * * * * * * * * * * * * * *

Bonus Tip: Touch Your Head

Instead of standing up for the interview, pairs remain seated and the talker puts her hand on the top of her head while answering the interview question. Again, the action creates smiles and keeps the answers short. Almost any motion or body part can be used!

Bonus Tip: Stretch It Out

Instead of standing on one leg, pairs stand and stretch while interviewing each other.

EACH ONE TEACH ONE

(Activity time: 1 – 2 minutes)

In **Presenting with Pizzazz,** I quote author Richard Bach who says:

We master what we teach.

So your learners need to teach what they've just learned to someone else.

In their expert groups, direct your learners to tell the others who they can share this information with – and how they plan to teach others what they've learned.

Give them some ideas: one-on-one discussions, coffee break or lunch chats, staff meetings, special meetings or classes, around the family dinner table, when playing golf or jogging, etc. Then let them take a minute to plan their own follow-up strategies.

**By making a verbal commitment
to tell someone else about what they learned,
learners will review the information again,
and remember it longer.**

* * * * * * * * * * * * * * * * * * *

Bonus Tip: Find That Person

Instead of an expert group discussion, learners stand and shout out the name of the person they plan to share the information with (example: co-worker, boss, students, family member, friend, etc.). Then they form standing groups with others who shouted out the same words. They tell their standing group members how they plan to teach others what they learned.

Bonus Tip: Just Do It

If your presentation involved learning a skill, now is the time to direct your learners to pair up and teach each other the skill – or have them model it for each other.

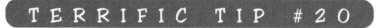

SING ALONG

(Activity time: 2 – 4 minutes)

Here are some other quick, high-energy ways to reconnect learners to each other and to invite them to celebrate the learning with you.

If they have been a part of an expert group, now is the time for them to thank their group members for their participation and to give each person in their group a high-five. They can also tell their group members what they plan to do with what they've learned.

They can create a group cheer and, when you count three, everyone in the room stands and gives their group cheers all at once. Or each group can do its group cheer individually.

They can stand and give those around them a handshake and comment ("Nice going! Good luck! Nice to have met you!").

Or you can have everyone stand and do a whole group cheer with you – maybe something topic related or maybe a group "wave."

How about a group song – one everyone knows and can sing with lots of energy and great gusto?

They'll leave high on the energy of the group – and on your unforgettable presentation!

* * * * * * * * * * * * * * * * * * * *

Bonus Tip: On the Wall

Before they leave the room, learners write their action plans on post-it notes and stick the notes to the door or wall near the door as they walk out. You can collect and read their action plans later. Or you can ask them for feedback on the post-it notes.

Bonus Tip: Ticket Out

Explain to the group that each person has to give you a ticket to get out the door. The ticket is an index card explaining one of the following:

➤ What they plan to do with what they learned;

➤ What they liked best about the lecture or presentation;

➤ What they want to learn next;

➤ A suggestion, comment, or idea they have about the talk or the topic.

Alive Again!

When love and skill work together, expect a masterpiece.

John Ruskin

You're on your way! With your enthusiasm, your passion, and your own special spirit, you're getting your message out to others so that they hear it. And now you're going to add the powerful piece that makes what you know even more memorable to your listeners – INVOLVEMENT. Because you're going to involve them while they're listening, you're helping your listeners LEARN and REMEMBER what they hear. This means that they'll USE it too, in some fashion, in their own lives. And of course, because they'll remember and use it, what naturally follows is that THEY'LL TEACH IT TO OTHERS.

By adding learner-involvement to your lecture, you're changing lives!

Take a moment to applaud yourself for this effort. The pat on the back that you give yourself isn't about ego. It isn't about delivering the perfect lecture. It isn't really about you at all. The applause you give yourself is because you are honoring your listeners in ways they are seldom honored. By involving them in their learning, you let them know that who they are and what they already know matters. You let them know that what they plan to do with what they learn from you matters too. ***You're helping them connect and grow as human beings even while they stretch their minds in new directions.***

You're doing even more than that:

> ***You're giving your listeners***
> ***an opportunity to share***
> ***their own ENERGY and SPIRIT***
> ***with you and with each other.***

You're allowing them to leave even richer than when they first came to you – richer with the new wisdom they gain and richer because of the interpersonal connections they make.

Instead of dying from the spoken word – the metaphorical demise many folks have experienced in the past – you're offering your listeners a new way to learn.

> ***You're bringing life back into their learning.***

You're changing them from mute listeners to involved learners – and they love you for it!

> ***So rejoice and be glad!***
> ***Your learners are awake, alert,***
> ***and alive because of you!***

A Final Thought

It was a chance conversation with a young man that pushed me over the edge – and onto the pages of this book. He was new to corporate training, eager and very professional in his black suit and muted tie. We stood for a few minutes in the middle of the ebb and flow of about 8,000 other conference participants. The occasion? The Training '01 Conference and Expo in Atlanta – one of the largest annual corporate training conferences in the country. Since we were both wearing presenter's badges, I asked him about his session topic.

"Interactive learning and audience participation," he replied.

"Wonderful! And what kinds of activities will your session participants be doing?" I continued.

"Oh no, there's no time to do activities. I have too much information to cover," he protested. "I'm just going to tell them about the activities I've created."

I was startled. Then I mentally excused his youth and inexperience and gently suggested, "Perhaps you may want to include one activity using some of your great material. After all, they will probably only remember 20% of what you say, but if you have *THEM* say and do something – however briefly – with your information, you can be assured that they'll remember closer to 90% of what you want them to learn."

He was adamant. "Nope, that would take up far too much time. I'll just tell them what they need to know. That way I can cover all the material."

My thoughts as I wished him good luck and melted into the flow of people? How sad – for him and for his session participants.

For him, because he was so unaware of how people really learn and how ineffective "telling" is.

For his session participants, because the important information that he had to give them would only be remembered by those few people who learn from and thrive on lecture. The rest would struggle to listen – and perhaps even struggle to stay awake.

Ah, but what if that young man had a collection of short, quick activities at his fingertips? Activities that took up no more than one or two minutes of his lecture time? Activities designed to keep his listeners awake and involved while he presented his information?

So this book came into being – with that young man in mind. And I also wrote it for all of us who, although we may be quite good at what we do, still need a reminder now and then:

The best way to make sure
our listeners learn, remember,
and use what we teach them,
is to involve them in the learning.

YOU are vitally important to your listeners – and so is your message. When you deliver it with your own passion and enthusiasm – AND when you involve your listeners – you create learning experiences that are absolutely unforgettable.

After all, many of them will never learn from anyone else what you have to give them. They are waiting for YOU. As **A Course in Miracles** states:

> **When the teacher is ready,**
> **the students will come.**

YOU are that teacher. So keep on polishing your teaching skills. Use your own wonderful talents, add to what you already know, share your energy and spirit with others, and enjoy every moment of the journey.

With cheers and blessings – and much love.

Sharon Bowman
Lake Tahoe
August, 2001

With Deepest Thanks

This book would not have been written were it not for the help and encouragement, and prayers of a number of special people:

Ross Barnett, my wonderful life partner, who is tireless in his support, and who lightens up my life with his humor;

Frances Bowman (my mom), who loves me, and who has always helped me make all my dreams come true;

Jan Thurman, my soul-sister and best friend, who "holds the note" for me, no matter what the external reality is;

Laura Moriarty, whose special friendship and "Sprouts" creativity meetings I treasure;

Gene Critchfield and Joyce Duvall, who took the time to give me feedback, and whose loving spirits are always close even though they live halfway across the country;

Karen Hewett, Debi Peterson, Diane Cheatwood, Cynthia Barnes – my dear Colorado family – for their energy and support;

Jim and Barb Weems, Ad Graphics owners and creators of book magic;

Peter Janzen, for his whimsical artwork and wonderful energy;

And all the folks I have talked with about alternatives to lecture.

About Sharon

Meet Sharon Bowman, your guide-on-the-side. She doesn't lecture. She doesn't expect you to sit, listen, and take notes.

Instead, through your involvement in hands-on learning activities, Sharon guarantees that you and your audiences will learn, remember, and use everything you hear, see, say, and do.

Sharon has been an author, teacher, trainer, and consultant for thirty years. She works with people who want to fine-tune their information-delivery skills, and companies that want to offer exceptional in-house training programs. She is a workforce development and Fortune 500 trainer, as well as a state and community college adjunct faculty member.

Sharon is also the director of **The Lake Tahoe Trainers Group,** an informal association of teachers, trainers, and consultants in and around the Lake Tahoe area. She is a member of the **National Speakers Association** and the owner of **Bowperson Publishing Company.** She is the author of three other popular teaching and training books.

You can contact Sharon at:

The Lake Tahoe Trainers Group
P.O. Box 564, Glenbrook, NV 89413
Phone: 775-749-5247
Fax: 775-749-1891
Email: SBowperson@aol.com
Web Site: www.Bowperson.com

SHARON'S BOOKS

Sharon's three popular "how-to" books are used by teachers, trainers, public speakers, presenters, human resource staff, and parents all across the country. See the descriptions below, or log onto **www.Bowperson.com** for more information.

ISBN 0-9656851-3-6 • $17.95

Shake, Rattle and Roll!

Toys, gadgets and gizmos, movement and metaphor. From simple, ordinary things, you can create extraordinary learning experiences for your students, audiences, and training participants. With *Shake, Rattle and Roll*, you'll discover over one hundred ways to make learning come alive with energy, excitement, meaning and memory.

How To Give It So They Get It!

Explore the ways you learn, teach, train, and give information to others. With easy-to-follow instructions for forty experiential training activities, *How To Give It So They Get It* will have you soaring with fresh ideas and renewed enthusiasm for teaching anyone anything and making it stick!

ISBN 0-9656851-2-8 • $17.95

ISBN 0-9656851-0-1 • $14.95

Presenting with Pizzazz!

This book gives you a host of easy-to-apply tips and activities for getting learners of all ages more actively involved in their own learning. Based on accelerated learning research and written in a fun, conversational style, *Presenting with Pizzazz* is a resource gem for today's busy teachers, trainers, and public speakers.

Sharon's books can be special ordered through your local bookstore, by using the following phone numbers or web sites, or by calling **Bowperson Publishing** at 775-749-5247.

The Trainers Warehouse: 800-299-3770
www.trainerswarehouse.com

The Humor Project: 518-587-8770
www.humorproject.com

The Bob Pike Group
Creative Training Techniques, Int'l.
800-383-9210
www.bobpikegroup.com

The Brain Store: 800-325-4769
www.thebrainstore.com

www.amazon.com
www.barnesandnoble.com
www.borders.com

Preventing Death By Lecture is also available for Christian communities under the title: *If Lazarus Did It, So Can You! Resurrecting The Learning In Your Churches, Schools, and Homes.* You can special order it through Christian bookstores and selected web sites and catalogs (call 775-749-5247 for ordering information).

CONFERENCE SESSIONS, KEYNOTES, AND TRAINING

Sharon offers a variety of interactive, learner-centered workshops and training for both in-house and public programs. Everything she designs and delivers is customized to fit the needs of the learners. A few of Sharon's popular seminar topics and interactive keynotes include:

Teach It Quick And Make It Stick! Creating Dynamic Learning Experiences for the Adult Learner.

Help! My Job is Driving Me Crazy! A Fresh Look at Managing Stress.

There's More To it Than Meets The Eye! Diversity in the Workplace.

Different Strokes for Different Folks! Working Together Through Changing Times.

I See What You Say! Worktalk in the Workplace.

Presenting with Pizzazz! Creating Fun and Memorable Meetings, Presentations, and Training.

For a complete list of titles, descriptions, availability, and cost options, please contact Sharon directly at: 775-749-5247. Or email her at: SBowperson@aol.com. Send your fax number or address and she can send you a packet of services, resources, and training information.

FAVORITE RESOURCES

Web Sites:

www.Bowperson.com – **Sharon Bowman's Web Site.** Of course this is Sharon's favorite – and it just might be yours! Sharon includes bimonthly updates of terrific tips, activities, and ideas from her own training experiences, as well as those of her readers. Also included are resources, special training events, and more about Sharon's books.

www.thebrainstore.com – **The Brain Store.** Products related to the brain and learning; a monthly web site newsletter of leading-edge brain/mind research; seminar information, new products and free samples.

www.alcenter.com – **The Center for Accelerated Learning.** The leading trainer of trainers in accelerated learning systems for organizations worldwide; products, seminars, tips, and links.

www.cttbobpike.com – **Creative Training Techniques, Int'l.** Custom train-the-trainer seminars featuring participant-centered learning; catalog products; free information.

www.humorproject.com – **The Humor Project.** Programs, products, daily doses and weekly wonders, free sourcebook, and vital signs.

www.thiagi.com – **Workshops by Thiagi, Inc.** Great web site that provides useful content without decorative flash; freebies and goodies; what's new; downloadable newsletters; products and services.

www.trainerswarehouse.com – **The Trainers Warehouse.** Fun, useful, and unusual products and ideas for presenters, trainers, sales people teachers – anyone who does presentations.

Newsletters:

Accelerated Learning Application News (262-248-7070). Editor: Tom Meier. Publisher: The Center for Accelerated Learning. Although the newsletter is no longer being printed, you can purchase all the back issues for a minimal fee. This is the most practical and usable newsletter for trainers and teachers of any content area – packed with how-to ideas, tips, and techniques as well as excellent updates on accelerated learning. A must for any trainer.

Creative Training Techniques Newsletter (800-707-7749). Editor: Bob Pike. Publisher: Lakewood Publications. Another great newsletter for trainers who want practical ideas that can be used immediately with little preparation time.

Catalogs:

The Brain Store Catalog (800-325-4769). Products and services on teaching, learning, and brain research; also includes some unusual brain-related items.

Creative Training Techniques Catalog (800-383-9210). An assortment of books and learning aids; especially for the busy trainer who wants some shortcuts in preparation time.

The Humor Project (518-587-0362). Upbeat items and books to help trainers add fun to their information delivery.

Jossey-Bass/Pfeiffer Catalog (800-274-4434). A large variety of books, VHS tapes, and other training resources.

Kipp Brothers Catalog (800-426-1153). A huge assortment of wholesale toys with great quantity pricing.

Lakeshore Learning Materials (800-421-5354). Supplier of children's educational toys including "Model Magic," a unique white sculpting material participants can write on.

Oriental Trading Company (800-228-2269). Unusual toy and craft items that can be bought in bulk.

The Trainer's Warehouse Catalog (800-299-3770). A fun and eclectic collection of products especially selected and developed to make training more hands-on and learner-centered.

Books:

Accelerated Learning CourseBuilder. The Center for Accelerated Learning, WI 1999 (262-248-7070)

Bowman, Sharon. ***Shake, Rattle and Roll.*** Bowperson Publishing, NV 1999 (775-749-5247)

Bowman, Sharon. ***How To Give It So They Get It.*** Bowperson Publishing, NV 1998

Bowman, Sharon. ***Presenting with Pizzazz.*** Bowperson Publishing, NV 1997

Cambell, William, Editor. ***New Paradigms for College Teaching.*** Interaction Book Company, MN 1997 (612-831-9500)

Charles, G. Leslie and Clarke-Epstein, Chris. *The Instant Trainer.* McGraw-Hill, NY 1998 (715-842-2467)

Hart, Leslie. *Human Brain and Human Learning.* Books for Educators, AR 1983

McCarthy, Bernice. *About Learning.* Excel, Inc., IL 1995

Meier, David. *The Accelerated Learning Handbook.* McGraw-Hill, NY 2000 (262-248-7070)

One Approach – With Style. The Community College of Aurora, CO (call Bowperson Publishing at 775-749-5247 for ordering information)

Rose, Colin. *Accelerated Learning for the Twentieth Century.* Dell Publishing, NY 1997

Silberman, Mel. *101 Ways to Make Training Active.* Jossey-Bass/Pfeiffer, CA 1995

Slan, Joanna. *Using Stories and Humor: Grab Your Audience.* Allyn & Bacon, MA 1998 (800-356-2220)

Thiagarajan, Sivasailam. *Facilitators Tool Kit.* (812-332-1478)